be good.
and the goodness

will come.

it has been
a brutal
few years

of learning
how to trust

myself.

broken people
might not mean

to hurt you

but they might
scratch you
with rough edges
all the same.

but love
is like water.
it softens everything

over time.

realizations come in waves.
we're never going to make it
to Nashville.

today you said it was a

white
hot
attraction

between us.
and that it was dangerous.

part of me wanted to apologize.
wanted to explain
it wasn't us.

it's just me.

and I wish I'd thought to warn you.

but I've always burned like this.

tonight I scrubbed everything in my bathroom
until it was white
and my lips went numb from the  fumes.

I will scrub my brain the same way.

it will be good and clean and forget
there was ever a time
before
or after
being happy.

people are lying
when they say life gets better
as you get older.

things pretty much don't change.

but you.

you
get better

if
you want to.

yesterday
I drank a drink
I can't pronounce

slumped on the floor

listening to records
I would never play
for myself.

and I thought
this is love.

this is being
with somebody.

but here I am.
still
quite alone.

what some people read
as sadness

others read
as relief

that they
are not alone.

these
are my people.

they know my heart.
they know my bones.

the quiet
and darkness
of my empty
apartment

greets me

like cool sheets

on a hot summer
night.

more.

but what about
the way

my calf
feels

skimming yours?

you crossed a room
to say hello
and

I couldn't think

of
a way
to explain

that my heart
wasn't
home.

the thing
about winter
is that

I get
to wear
my armor

outside

of my skin.

"I think there is something very wrong with me."

"I think it's funny."

more.

learning
to love

comes
in waves.

let them
wash you

clean.

It has been 42 days since
some body

has touched me.

it
is getting harder
to remember.

it
is no one's fault
that you don't love me.

more.

"I'm afraid of being loved."

"no,
you're afraid that loss
is inevitable."

it's strange to think
I'm eating breakfast

with you

in the same place
you were shot.

"things change," you say.

things change.

more.


on a lighter note.

you're now
the second man
I've kissed goodbye
in
this diner.

I guess
this is home now.

it is natural to wish
for more
or less

of the things
that hurt
or heal
you.

but it is useless.
remember
that
too.

what does it sound like
when you sing?

like everything
that's happened
is happening

again.

more.

it is tough
to remember
your heartache
isn't

my heartache
too.

how do smokers cope

when
it rains?

more.

my heart
is fighting
to stay

undone.

you loved me
like

I have always
been bigger
than
myself.

more.

I fell into you
like
a bad habit

over
and over
and over

again.

if they make
choices

not
to love you.


leave.
let them go.

don't look back.

tastebuds change
every thirty days
but

how many
more

to wash
you
from my blood?

forks scrape against empty plates
and cans hiss
as we crack them.

but mostly,
we eat in silence.
shuffling around
all the things

we're trying to remember
not to talk

about.

more.

sometimes I forget how to love myself.

and then I spend a week in the bath.
guzzling water. soaking in salt. pumicing feet.
slathering oil.

I scrub and I clean and I polish.

until I am pink and moist and happy all over.

later, lying in bed, one very soft foot will run itself
across the sole of the other.

and then, I will remember.

you said
"your body is just like Barbie.
it's awesome,
almost like plastic."

almost
like not even a person
at all.

more.

selfies are my favorite form of self expression.

closely followed by screaming into the abyss.

most days I wake up
and just want to move
to Florida.

it seems like America's
last great frontier
and sinking ship.

all in one.

more.

skin pressed
against skin

no room
left

for doubt

between
us.

it's important
to remember

even
sweet words

can hold you.
hostage.

more.

I am
more
important
than
pretty.

please stop
asking me to be smaller.

please stop
asking for things
that would break me
to give.

more.

I'm tired
of being written
off

as a bitter bitch.
like it's not right

that I'm angry.

I am a person, not a prop.
I am a person, not a prop.
I am a person, not a prop.
I am a person, not a prop.
I am a person, not a prop.
I am a person, not a prop.
I am a person, not a prop.
I am

more.

it is
a ring of hell

not to trust

the same people
as
you love.

correct this.
and live.

whiskey and
sadness.

shouldn't
mix.

more.

if it's any
consolation

I don't expect
to get

you
either.

I'm afraid
I will clean
the dishes
and
fold my clothes

and you will
still
not love me.

more.

I miss the summer.

I had
three boyfriends.

and so little time
to worry.

you don't need
to be tough

all the time.

it isn't weak
to cry.

every body
is a garden.

loosen that heart
and water
yours.

more.

not everyone
will love you.

for being strong.

it's okay.
you don't need them.

you are strong.

we only
have sex
when we're drunk.

it's the only time
you make me
laugh

anymore.

success has ruined
so many men
I've loved.

failure
would have too.

it's just time
and change
after
us all.

stop
looking

for a place
to put
your heart.

you are
your own home.

the guilt.
of not
asking.

could eat you
alive.

can we
stop
pretending

you didn't

set my home
on fire

and
ask me
why it burns?

more.

love wasn't meant
to hurt.

who
never
told you
that?

you kiss
my thighs.

I grab
your chin.

you ask forgiveness.
I don't give in.

more.

can you still
taste
her?

you stopped asking

to peek through
my windows

as if
unaware

the view
kept
changing.

more.

not every conversation
is asking
to be
understood.

a letter to my mother:

I'm sorry.
that I ever asked

you

to be softer.

more.

I love to walk home
at night
and
pass
only women.

it is nice
to feel safe.

## DEAR STRANGER

I will not feel
sorry

that feeling safe
is
more important

(to me)

than you feeling trusted.

if you don't see
why

what I'm doing
is
important.

that's okay.

you
don't have to.

"I really liked him."

"you really like them all until you don't."

our thighs were touching and he asked to put his arm around me.

I said yes.

he did.

and then he said I can't remember what I was saying.

I felt my brain go numb while he touched me for the first time.

he smiled and said I feel like that's okay.

are you
happy though?

your body is a stream.
I just want to run

my fingers
through
and through
and through

again.

sydney boyle

it is early
in morning
and
everything

still too tender
to touch.

more.

sometimes even
my
coffee

tastes like
empty

sex
and sadness.

he held me so closely I felt his skin meld into mine.

I said "don't let go."

he said "never."

more.

sometimes
I cry
when we're together

because even
with
your fingers locked
into mine.

I can't seem to reach you.

why
the fuck

are we both

so afraid.

more.

me, you
and everyone
I have ever loved.

it is not your fault
that you don't love me.

it is your fault
that you tried to convince me
that you did.

you can't understand
why

I'm still upset.

it's because
I was raised
with the guilt of knowing

if you left,

it's because I failed.
to make you want
to stay.

brick by brick,
thought by thought,
I'm dismantling everything

you ever taught
me.

more.

I used to tell him, "you're not really in love with me.
you're in love with an idea of me."

and he always got so angry.

"what kind of shit is that? of course you fall in love with
the idea of a person. that's all we are to each other --
ideas."

but he saw me then.
long
before

I saw myself.

I didn't cry
when I read
that you were gone.

I lost my fucking mind.

more.

can I please
stop pretending
it's okay?

I can not stand
the stillness

of whatever
 is coming

next.

more.

everything
feels
like riding through
an open stretch
of scorched road.

with your hand
on my thigh.
just

a little too fast
to enjoy.

I just want to kiss
your face

to remind you.

it's okay.

more.

settle down.

it will come.

their success
is not
your failure.

more.

summer comes
like cherries
on my tongue.

hands on my hips.

and I forget
the sadness
ever
lived.

I don't really know
if heaven exists
or
what it means

but

I like to think
that I'm nice
and they'd probably let me in.

more.


sometimes

freedom
looks
like accepting.

they don't need to understand.

it is a full moon.
and I feel my body
hungry.

for everything
that was ever

taken.

you say,
that my hair is long
and
my skin is dark.

a lot of things have changed.

you touch my lip
and
remind me.

a lot of things
haven't.

I feel my love
flooding the room.

dripping
from the ceiling fan.
flowing everywhere.

but into
you.

and your mouth looks so dry,
but tears can't quench
it.

you need water.
and I can't
seem to be
anything

but salt.

I pull your cheek
to my shoulder.
lace my fingers
through your hair.
wrap my legs around
your waist.
and hope.

that this is enough.

that my touch,
that my love,
is enough.

for your body
to stop hurting

itself.

I ran out of ways
to explain

the way that I love you.

but we both know
I do.

I think happiness
will be

the day
I can sit quietly
and stop

asking myself why.

learn to be here.

here is what you have.

more.


I had no idea I would be happy

until I was.

some people
just say "I love you" after
but we

we prefer to say
"we probably shouldn't have done that."
and not speak
for a week
instead.

more.

someone's inability
to see

your value

doesn't change
your worth.

it is not your fault
they were too drunk
to love
you.

it's not your fault
they were to drunk
to care.

you brought me pizza
and kissed me politely
and gave me pajamas
and held me close
as we slept.

and I think
I will love you.

even if it doesn't last.

and you kiss my fat lips
with yours.
what does it taste like?

honey
and blood,
you say.
honey and blood.

I grab your face from between my
spread.
kiss your fat lips
with mine.

honey and blood,
I say.
honey and blood.

you sleep beside me.
but I feel you

in my bones.

how?

fuck
what they call
women

like me.

I don't owe
you

an explanation

of my own
crooked teeth.

I hate the way
you say my name
like

it is
a word.

and not a song.

more.

I am
everything
you love

about
a home
you don't call
home

anymore.

you told me
I made you soft.
made you gentler.

that you needed
piss

and
vinegar.

so now
you only
kiss me
sweetly

in dark rooms.

when we're drunk.

and no one
is watching.

I feel like a thousand sunny days
strung together

and other things

you can't touch.

what if I touched
your body

while I used words
like pillaged
and destroyed
and smashed
to describe
it.

would you believe me?
when I promised
that I never meant
to hurt

you.

you
tell yourself
you don't love me.

and I
never tell you.

I disagree.

not all of us know
we are worth good things.

today I worried
about the meaning of life.

but don't worry.
my friend Ben,

told me it's sex.

I place water at your plate
and you don't drink it.

I look at your lips
cracked
and dry
and thirsting.

you don't drink it.

I look at your lip.
it's bleeding.

I look at your lip
and wonder.

how could you know
how to care

for me?

it's hard not to feel
the weight.

of my existence.

in
unpaid
dollar bills.

you asked me
what happiness was like
so I closed
your eyes

and kissed your lids until you screamed.

what I want most,
is a cocktail
on a patio
in a short skirt

and a strangers hand
on my bare thigh
just to remind you
(and I)
that I can.

but I love you.
so I don't.

more.

sometimes I spend time with you
and it feels like punishment
for having missed you.

stop telling me
that
I changed
you.

for the better.
for all the women
after me.

I am not just a lesson.
in your journey
to happiness.

I am a woman.

you failed.
to love.

more.

you
do not
have to be
a door

for every soul
seeking

shelter.

be gentle
with yourself.

it is how you learn.

love is not
a sweet nectar.

it is water.

in
your blood.

without it
you fail

to live.

stop
looking
for drinks
in

the desert.

more.

I wanted
to be better than this.

I am tired.
I am scared.
I am small.

but loving you
was a strength
built

into
my bones.

you don't know
what
you want.

stop punishing
me
by pretending you do.

I remember
the first time
my brothers
explained butter-faces to me.

"she's hot
everywhere 'but-her' face"

they explained to me.

"it's not mean,
it's funny.
it's not like
we're saying it to someone."

they said to me.

I looked down at my hands and
prepubescent body
and wondered.
how many men might someday like

to sever
my  face from
my body.

more.

they
didn't know.

the ones
who say
they don't deserve you
usually don't.

more.

let go
of things
that hurt you.

I am done
with
being told.

to wait
for success

and happiness

quietly.

happy.

and so very
alone.

I watch your eyes.
and wait.
as your wrongs

un-do
themselves.

more.

I want
things
I haven't
seen.

I'm still trying
to learn the difference

between skin
and
forgiveness.

more.

I'm sorry

I thought the answer
was to hit.

harder.

sometimes I like to look around my room at all the things I've kept longer than men. I pet my desk and cuddle my lamp and say, "see, I can care for you. you aren't afraid of where we are going and neither am I."

but I hate to look at the wine.

the wine never lasts.

I never needed you.

it was always, only, ever
want.

my skin sticks
to everything it touches.
the porch, itself, your hands,
the heat.

your voice drowns in
cicadas,
commuter trains
and your loud mouth neighbors.

summer comes
like
relief.

you pull me close.
put your nose
against
my hair.

and I wonder

can you still smell
him there?

this man
won't stop.

it's like
he can't see

your fingerprints
still across

my lips.

the air is heavy with water.
waiting.

to fall.
like it knows.

I need forgiveness.

give
yourself
permission.

more.

you owe
yourself
more.

his lips
don't taste

like
yours.

but they say
so many,
good things

too.

I'm afraid to fall
in love.
I'm afraid of being
open.
I'm afraid of death and wasted efforts.

but

I keep putting clothes on
and hoping

for the best.

my skin is on fire
my back
is in knots

and everything
still tastes
like you.

I'm trying.

I swear I'm trying
to stay.

good.

I want to take you
in my hands.

pour honey on your limbs
until you are sticky
and ripe.

I want to wash you
with milk.

rub sea salt across
your back
your chest
your calves
and feet.

rub
until your heart

feels tender.
and raw.
and new.

and that big hand
just wrapped itself
around
my wrist.

just as I began to forget.

tender things
still exist.

you keep painting
palm trees
and oil
fires

and swear.

somehow.

you're not thinking of me.

you think
I should walk a little quieter.
and act a little more grateful
that you allow
me

to exist.


I won't.

I used to date this older guy
who liked to not invite me out
and show up at my doorstep drunk at 3 a.m.

he showed up one night and threw 37 magnets
at my fridge door until they all stuck.

then he wrapped his big arms around me
and said, "it's not your fault that you're so dumb."

that summer
I found long walks
and Italian ice.

they have been
my solace.

ever since.

I started writing because my mom told me I needed more creative ways of saying fuck you.

I found them.

I could write you a list
of all the things
I'm not sorry
for.

but it would never end.

I love you

but
love,

is not enough.

more.

you say things to me gently.
you say things to me twice.

you came to me
softly.
you came here
to stay.

I look at your big hands,
those strong arms,
so close
to my throat.

and I think
what a miracle.

to love a man.
that does not make me fear.

add lemon to your water.
charcoal to your teeth.
honey to your skin.

cleanse, then cleanse
and cleanse.

why don't we feel
clean?

you read something
and it changes you

and you're afraid
because you don't know

how.

I keep wondering
what I would look like
as somebody
you could have
loved.

I think my hair
would be wilder
and I would be taller.
and my laughter

my laughter
would sounds like mountains
knocking.

if you knew

you
wouldn't

have
to ask.

we spent a summer
avoiding

all the same things.

together.

a man I liked cancelled our date on the walk home tonight.

he told me it wasn't me as a group of men crowded closer to me and yelled "nice ass."

I just want to be a person.

I just want to be loved.

in that order of importance.

I smell like freedom
and everything
else

you forgot how
to love.

sometimes
there is nothing

to do

but
wait

for the poison
to clear.

I scrub last night's
dishes.

sage
the windows
and the doors.

straighten, tidy and wipe
until everything
looks new.
and untouched.

close my eyes
and
realign.

you were never here.

my hobbies include
getting drunk
and reminding people I love them.

also dancing.
sober.

more.

no chill.
but
a lot of good intentions.

I'll just be here
licking
the tips of glasses

and forgetting

how to drink.

if they don't
laugh
at your jokes

run.

I'm hiding behind
34 canvases
leaking colors
you hate.

they all smell
like you.

my pigments
mixed
with yours.

a mess

I can't seem
to undo.

more.

my heart
feels a bit empty

now
that it has forgotten.

missing
you.

punishing them
will punish
you too.

more.

I'm not afraid
of you
 not coming back.

Made in the USA
Columbia, SC
10 July 2018